Dr. Michal Schanin & Vera Yogev

Between the Lines

Developing Strategic Reading Skills
Instruction | Learning | Alternative Assessment

Workbook 2

Senior Editors & Producers: Contento
Translation: Naama Meron-Asher
Editing: Gayla Goodman
Book Design: Liliya Lev Ari

Copyright © 2016 by Dr. Michal Schanin & Vera Yogev and Contento

All rights reserved. No part of this book may be translated, reproduced, stored in a retrieval system or transmitted, in any form or by any means, electronic, photocopying, recording or otherwise, without prior permission in writing from the author and publisher.

ISBN: 978-965-550-516-0

International sole distributor: Contento
22 Isserles Street, 6701457 Tel Aviv, Israel

www.ContentoNow.com
Netanel@contento-publishing.com

Dr. Michal Schanin & Vera Yogev

Between the Lines

*Developing Strategic Reading Skills
Instruction | Learning | Alternative Assessment*

Workbook 2

Table of Contents

Introduction 7

    1. The Maid 28

    2. The Sparrow 36

    3. The Three Counsels of the Rooster 47

    4. Not to Shame 57

    5. Small Fish, Big Fish 71

    6. The Bundle of Sticks 78

Assessment Tools 83

    1. Alternative Assessment — Indicator of Reading and Comprehension on Three Levels of Thinking 83

    2. Learning Journal 87

Tables of Graded Language Patterns 93

Table of Workbook 2 Texts and Skills 98

Introduction

When one delves into the professional literature about reading, one might come across many publications on this subject. However these articles might not offer a satisfying explanation about the process of acquiring reading.

In the past, a common and prevailing belief maintained that if students were to be confronted with questions about the content of the text, eventually they would understand its meaning independently. Yet today it is widely accepted that the extent and depth of reading processes are not as simple as that.

The process of extracting meaning out of texts encompasses various aspects. Take, for example, producing meaning out of the text and augmenting, assessing and creating new meanings out of this text. It turns out that acquiring the meaning of a text is not restricted only to processing information, finding answers and the automatic output of deciphering text. In contrast, acquiring the meaning of a text is a complex multi-dimensional process.

Every reader can achieve and develop a process of producing meaning from the text, and in this way exercise beneficial skills and strategies that help understand the meaning. Therefore, teachers should instruct their students in ways to pair skills and strategies to various reading situations while relying on syntactic, semantic and pragmatic clues in order to extract meaning from a text.

The development of reading and the production of meaning from a text happen simultaneously to many other interrelated skills. Readers often find that their involvement in the reading process and in the grapho-phonemic deciphering process assists their capability to understand the context. These skills guide children through the deciphering process. Simultaneously, it provides them with feedback as to the extent of correctness achieved by their deciphering.

Reading is an interactive process that interrelates many and varied skills. To achieve skilled reading, one must develop reading skills and strategies that may avail him or her during reading. Integral integration of the whole pack of strategies—deciphering and understanding while applying meta-cognitive checking—can lead readers to skilled reading. These reading skills serve as a toolbox for the readers and help them with reading and understanding texts. Skillful readers transform skills into an integral part of the process of reading. Thus for example, readers can understand the main idea of a text quickly and precisely, foretell coming events in the text, draw conclusions from a text and apply the meaning of the text to their own personal lives.

The skill of producing meaning from a text might become an automatic and unaware one, but using strategies is a result of a well-informed and intentional discretion: how to cope with reading tasks and which skills to use.

Pearson et al. (1990) emphasized in their research that not only the reader's skills but also the right timing is necessary. Both capabilities–the ability to plan reading and the right timing–create a productive result in achieving reading strategies and meta-cognitive control.

We have learned from our long-term work in the educational field that teachers need to put theoretical methods into practice. These skills and strategies are highly important in developing language education in the various populations of students.

We have chosen from the varied curriculum of language education a genre (system) that can demonstrate to teachers and students some core strategies. After becoming familiar with them, they can put them into practice.

Basic Hypotheses

* Language education takes on language both as a means and an end in developing students' language efficiency in oral and written language.

* Preschool children start their schooling geared with a wide and varied linguistic knowledge (mainly their proficiency of oral language) but also of written language. This knowledge is expressed through understanding and production of clauses and phrases and through the unique meanings a child may attach to them.

* One can detect a variance in the level of language acquisition among peers. This variance is manifested through the pace of acquiring reading, vocabulary, discourse styles, cognitive development and more.

* Written language can be challenging for the acquiring student; direction and explicit learning in class is needed to help students with this.

* The notion *language* refers to various communication channels and to different discourse styles as well as to varied levels of language and genres.
* The genre that was selected for this book specifically refers to folktales, fables and folklore.
* Knowledge of language may include both grammatical and practical proficiency and the know-how of using language in different contexts.
* The knowledge of language is acquired through textual contexts.
* By initially practicing patterns that consist of simple phrases in order to gradually acquire a language, the learner progresses to building up more complex sentences that he or she can grasp with the mind.

Aims of Language Education

A meta-aim of language education is to foster a literate person for whom language can meet with the reader's communicative needs:

* Producing meaning from written texts and maintaining a well-informed use of the unique genre we chose for this book.
* Providing tools and skills that deliver knowledge about language and learning strategies that will be acquired by using this specific genre and applying these tools, skills and strategies to other genres.
* Developing an informed reading ability of literary texts and Jewish folktales and maintaining a dialogue with Jewish sources.
* Developing students' capability of written expression, which allows them to express their inner and outer worlds.
* Learning the various usages of language: listening, speaking, reading and writing. These usages interrelate with skills that are involved with understanding and expressing language.
* Developing activities that foster meta-linguistic knowledge about language (learning journal, indicators).

* Developing the ability to pass on knowledge through speech, writing and reading exercises.

* Handling texts while manipulating a structured learning of linguistic patterns (language patterns) in order to gear learners with various tools that allow self-expression, reading comprehension and critical, analytical and evaluation reading

The Goals of Language Education

* Development of skills and strategies that structure the meaning of the text while providing a toolbox that can help students through the reading process.

* Development of thinking skills in students through reading that spans from a verbal production of meaning to providing an applied meaning of a text.

* Development of language enrichment for students by gradually providing them with linguistic tools that can present them with the basics of meaningful reading.

* Development of retrieving and matching capabilities in students that enable them to match various strategies and skills to varied types of texts.

* Development of capabilities in students to transform various strategies and apply them correctly in all types of texts in Hebrew learning environments such as history, Bible, geography, etc.

* Development of appreciation and control processes in students, which are based on indicators. These indicators are a part of the criteria that belong to each strategy.

* Development of reflection and feedback in students about all processes of learning, thinking, and reading while using a learning journal that documents their reading.

* Enhancing teachers' capabilities of mediating between text and reader. At the same time, adjusting skills and reading strategies that facilitate a meaningful understanding of the text.

* Enhancing the teacher's skill of establishing various independent tasks at different thought levels, following the example molded by this workbook.

Enhancing the teacher's awareness of the passages, scaling up from literate to interpretive understanding. Directing a teacher's attention to differences that might exist among the students in the class. Principles of the Program

The program focuses on the control of managing literacy in discourse, which enables speakers to adjust their language to social circumstances and aims, to various knowledge areas and to their previous knowledge of a target population. The language education curriculum aims to cover various texts that belong to genres and sub-genres of varied fields of knowledge. Literacy functioning is the ability to understand different genres and use them in oral conversation. In this program we chose one genre in particular. We formulated six texts for each age group. Our program deals with the full literate discourse that is very characteristic of tales, fables and folktales. Being part of the curriculum, this choice intends to meet with two of our aims: first to practice language and then to help with the production of meaning from texts. Students love and are willing to use this genre, and they find it fun and motivating personally and culturally. Our second aim is to enable students to learn a lesson from this genre. The program enhances the student's listening and oral expression skills. We also made sure to integrate these skills in various activities. The skill of developing listening abilities is an outcome of a constant dialogue that exists between the spoken and written discourses.

During the program, students are asked to listen to the teacher or their peers who read to them in front of the whole class. The workbook assignments are latterly practiced in groups or individually and at the end of the activity each group or individual presents their thoughts to the whole class.

The feedback—a learning journal will document their learning, enabling the students to follow up on the meta-cognitive processes.

By using these meta-cognitive processes, students may acquire both linguistic knowledge and may understand various genres and subgenres of texts.

The World of Discourse—The Genre: Legends, Tales and Fables

Legends, tales and fables all belong to one genre that provides insights into past or present events together with an added value of their cultural and authentic facets. The strict and set structure of this genre is based on its background, its characters and its lessons to be learned. In order to learn how to forge meaning out of these characteristics, learners are provided with strategies that reflect and focus on differences that exist in this genre and point to variances that can be found in the backgrounds, structures, messages, characters and their interactions with our tales.

The most prominent characteristic of this genre is its formal construction, which consists of introduction, setting, conflict, catharsis or peak, resolution, turning point and conclusion.

In order to understand the process in texts, an awareness must be raised in students to the sequence of the plot, its details and the characters. Students learn how to separate the wheat from the chaff, both orally and textually. To acquire these strategies students are dependent on their linguistic knowledge of verbs, adjectives, structural words and phrases, which altogether are very helpful in delivering the entire plot and subtexts.

Through reading the text, readers can establish their own personal interpretations and crystallize their attitudes to it; allowing them to make their own premises and draw conclusions that result in a critical reading of the text. All these traits are immensely helpful and ameliorate students' understanding of the text and help develop various skills.

In addition, readers format their own personal viewpoint of the text and can identify with the author's viewpoint.

Leading the learner to these outcomes should happen through practicing various and relevant learning strategies. At the same time learners must use appropriate language structures.

About the Program

Based on a cognitive approach, the underlying features of our program *Between the Lines* include using reading skills and strategies as well as harnessing the student's meta-cognitive system for directing and orienting reading (Pearson1990).

According to this approach there are seven principle characteristics that are shared by all skilled readers without regard to their level or age:

1. A reader can easily separate the wheat from the chaff.

2. Readers look for a link between material they know and newly read material.

3. A reader establishes a hypothetical model for the newly read themes; a model to be tested throughout reading.

4. The model established by the reader will be remodeled according to conclusions the reader draws from the meaning of the text.
5. A reader can summarize what she or he has just read.
6. A reader is efficient in drawing conclusions throughout and after the process of reading and can achieve full understanding of the text.
7. A reader can independently raise questions about the author, the text and themselves.

All these skills should be acquired by readers so they can potentially reach a better understanding of the text.

The *Between the Lines* program applies to three levels of thinking:
1. A literal understanding of the text.
2. An interpretative level of the text.
3. An implemental level of the text.

After being divided into sub-skills, these levels can be found helpful in creating intermediate stages in the process of reading and producing the text meaning. We developed our method through eclectic and integrative means and "implementation tools;" namely the above-mentioned skills and strategies that interweave through the three levels of understandings mentioned above. These implementation tools should meet with most of the needs of our student populations, including under-achieving populations and special-needs students. Our program has put an emphasis on linguistic enrichment and practice while paying attention to the deep structural layers of language and linguistic enrichment. This emphasis is manifested through the following implementation tools:

* Graded linguistic patterns.
* Implicit and explicit content clues.
* General and linguistic cloze excerpts.

The graded linguistic patterns are syntactical structures that provide the entire components of the English language.

Implicit and explicit content clues—provide accessories for the reader. Through locating these implicit and explicit content clues a student becomes an independent, skilled and efficient reader. The content clues allow him or her to unfold meaning and internal contexts of a sentence.

Cloze passages—texts that have blanks in them where some of the words in the texts are missing. By recovering the excerpt through embedding the omitted words, a student can test his or her proficiency by using the three above-mentioned levels of text understanding.

In order to be able to recover a deficient passage the student should command these skills: linguistic skills, the ability of contextual and textual repetition and pragmatic and cultural knowledge skills.

* Linguistic skills—includes vocabulary and syntax.
* Contextual ability—the links that tie together parts of a text.
* Pragmatic knowledge—former knowledge that can be applied.
* Cultural knowledge—a culture-dependent knowledge.

Our *Between the Lines* program integrates both tools of assessment and measuring that yield feedback and reflection to teachers about their methods of teaching, about their students' learning and student-teacher interrelated dialogue.

The two assessment tools that were selected for *Between the Lines* are:

1. Learning journal
2. Indicators

Both tools help to develop teacher-learner communication. They also contribute to formative assessment and summative assessment.

1. Learning Journal

A learning journal is one of the learning and assessment tools designed for acquiring knowledge through the raising of guided questions. It prompts the intrinsic self-searching of students and encourages them to look closely at their learning processes.

A learning journal can store all the linkages and products that were documented by learners throughout their learning processes. It offers an initial stock of learning processes.

By verbalizing their thinking processes, learners can raise awareness of their learning experiences. Journals can also provide them with fresh knowledge about their own learning and thinking strategies (Birnbaum, 1999). Learners can also retrospectively view their successes and challenges. Furthermore, verbalizing of thinking processes can help students enhance their potential for being "independent learners."

The components of our Learning Journal include:

* Addressing the gist of knowledge.
* Addressing and locating challenges.
* Finding a link between prior personal knowledge and current knowledge.
* Forming an opinion and taking a stand.

2. Indicators

An Indicator is based on yardsticks that familiarize students with what is expected of them throughout the upcoming assignments.

Each indicator manifests some dimensions, which are needed for giving indication about the quality of students' work. They can usually be further divided into three levels of student control and performance:

* At the beginning—students are without control.
* On their way to goal-achieving—are partly in control.
* Fully achieving their goal—are in full control.

The characteristics of these yardsticks apply to each of the above-mentioned levels of performance. By tracing these characteristics, teachers and students can diagnose the level of performance achieved and what should be improved and/or strengthened. In the same vein, these characteristics can point to weaknesses and strengths of the learning process.

The Indicator is a guiding light that students follow on their way to achieving their goals—control and strategy. These yardsticks present the students, in painstaking detail, the expectations of their performance. Success measures can mirror students' abilities and direct them to achieving higher levels of success.

By being a teacher-student interactive tool, the Indicator helps teachers continue to be persistent and accurate in their evaluations. By enabling students to realize their own challenges and strengths, the Indicator also raises awareness of their teacher's expectations and evaluations.

Design of the Program

This program is comprised of three workbooks that were especially designed for enhancing reading and thinking and for acquiring text meaning by way of implementing tools for self-evaluation and measuring for learners and teachers.

Aimed at 2nd to 6th graders and their teachers, the program can be modularly implemented by the teacher by matching the level of workbook to his or her class level, in full accord with students' needs.

The program allows teachers to choose and delegate various assignments to different students. Its underlying objective is to develop appropriate reading and writing skills in students that are needed for a versed usage of the written language.

By not aiming at specific student knowledge that was learned in class and by not testing it, the program alternatively provides students with skills they need for functional literacy. It also supports them in learning which skills and thinking strategies are needed for each specific literacy activity.

Each workbook contains a repository of six literary texts that were extracted from a widely-accepted curriculum for elementary schools. In each text, the three levels of thinking (verbal understanding, interpretive understanding and the implemental level) are practiced. There are sub-skills in each level of thinking that are also practiced, and all in all they are aimed at developing a meta-cognitive thinking ability that provides guidance for using the right tools. Each workbook contains an introduction that was written for teachers and parents, illuminating the principles and goals of the program.

Verbal Understanding

The level of verbal understanding includes the following skills:

Sequence

The narrative sequence is practiced in the current workbook through using:

1. A sequence of segments.
2. A sequence of key sentences.
3. A sequence of keywords.
4. A sequence of questions.

Workbook 1 places a special emphasis on the issue of sequential abilities. Sequence in narratives is a topic that has been thoroughly investigated in literature. It was found that when students achieve an understanding of the narrative sequence of a text they can also grasp more than 50 percent of the text content without dwelling on minute narrative details.

B. The Skill of Finding Detail

The skill of finding detail is practiced in this workbook by raising questions such as:

1. Who said this to whom?
2. Find an alternative word.
3. True or False?
4. Classification tables.

A reader can piece together the details of the narrative sequence by using this skill.

C. Locating a Main Idea

Locating a main idea is practiced in this workbook by locating a key sentence of the text that holds a wealth of keywords. Linking keywords by conjunctions will lead readers to the sentence that presents the main idea of the text.

D. Raising and Classifying Questions

Being a meta-cognitive skill, this ability is practiced in the workbook by using interrogatives, namely WH-words, in readers' three levels of thinking:

Literal level of questions	Interpretive level of questions	Implemental questions
Who?	Why?	What did you feel…?
What?	How?	What do you think…?
How much?	Whether?	What would you do instead…?
Where to?	Which?	Was the author right when…?
Where?	How come?	Why do you think it happened….?
Where?	In which way?	What would you do if…?

The practice of raising questions in these three levels of thinking and at the same time compiling them and classifying them in tables, supports the development of thinking in students.

E. Mapping out of Concepts

To exercise this skill we developed three tools for knowledge management. The beneficial aspect of these tools is that they allow for plotting graphical maps out of linear text. Using keywords and conjunctions and embedding them in these maps helps the student sum up the text.

The three tools of knowledge management are:

1. Flow charts.
2. Venn Diagrams.
3. Diffuse Mapping.

1. Flow Charts

Flow charts are helpful in tracking plots and sequences of events or can be used in scientific texts that are based on cause and effect.

By plotting a chart, a learner defends his or her understanding of the text. By embedding keywords and key sentences in a chart a learner manifests his or her ability to separate the wheat from the chaff.

Flow charts can also be utilized for developing the skill of summarization. This skill consists of using keywords and key sentences and of integrating conjunctions to make a link between them.

2. Venn Diagrams

This tool can be used in cases when we want to demonstrate contrast and to compare things (intersection and union). Embedding keywords and key sentences in these diagrams trains learners to separate the wheat from the chaff.

For example:

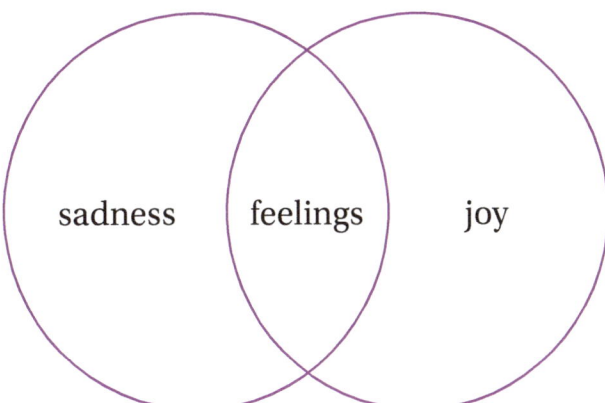

Through using Venn Diagrams, one can develop his or her summarization skills: joining together keywords and key sentences within the Venn diagram and then making a connection between them with a conjunction and creating a summarization out of them.

3. Concept Map

Using this mapping helps students to select factual information from informative texts, if the sequential order is irrelevant in these texts.

To organize this factual information a student can plot it in classification tablets that consist of columns of generalizing semantic categories. In this way items are grouped together under the same category. This tool for organizing information is selected according to the text genre.

F. Classification

This ability is practiced through using classification tables in the current workbook. Classification tables are information organizers. They are built by manipulating either inductive or deductive reasoning. In more simple words, the method of reasoning can derive general principles from particular facts or derive the reasoning by going from the general to the specific facts.

G. Separating the Wheat from the Chaff

To encourage students to practice this skill the workbook offers three principle tools:
1. Naming the sequence of segments.
2. Locating key sentences.
3. Locating keywords.

1. Naming the Sequence of Segments

The skill of naming the sequence of segments entails one to locate the meaningful segments of the narrative, to identify bridging passages between segments and to give titles for each segment separately. The resulting sequence of titles will yield a synopsis of the narrative.

2. Locating Key Sentences

The text key sentences are those that are most significant in each segment; sentences that without them a segment would be meaningless.

There are two main questions for locating and identifying key sentences in each segment.

a. Who is the segment talking about?

b. What is the segment talking about?

The answers to these questions might be either one or several key sentences of a text.

3. Locating Keywords

The text keywords are the main words in the sentence that if omitted in the sentence might cause the sentence to become meaningless. In order to locate keywords in a sentence we need to ask two questions:

a. Who is the sentence talking about?

b. What is the sentence talking about?

H. Linguistic Program

The linguistic-syntactic enrichment of our program is an integral part that integrates graded linguistic structures in most stories. We built up the linguistic training through various tools beginning from simple linguistic-syntactic patterns through to complex syntactical structures:

1. Graded linguistic patterns

2. Cloze

3. Explicit and implicit content clues

1. Graded linguistic patterns

Linguistic patterns are a sequence of syntactic structures that are gradually built up and accumulated: from simple to compound and complex sentences.

These syntactical structures are organized and graded according to a sequential development of language (see a continuum of linguistic patterns achieved at the end of workbook).

2. Cloze

A cloze is based on the meaning of the whole story but certain words are omitted from the text and the blanks create deficiencies in the integrity of the text.

This exercise allows readers to conjecture about the missing words and base their conjectures on the context of the text and by the way they understand its meaning. This ability can be achieved via three skills:

* Linguistic skill

- * Context and textual repetition
- * Linguistic skill + textual repetition and context + pragmatic knowledge

Linguistic skills—the ability to reconcile deficient text by repairing it with vocabulary from former linguistic and syntactic repertoire.

Context and textual repetition—the ability to pick out a word from the text and repeat it in the right context in order to reconcile the deficient text.

Linguistic ability + context and textual repetition + pragmatic knowledge—allows for recalling of former knowledge (cultural, linguistic and pragmatic knowledge) and thus it facilitates in completing a deficient sentence.

I. Explicit and Implicit Content Clues

The linguistic ability of locating implicit and explicit content clues helps learners to independently highlight meanings from the text and to become independent and skilled readers without becoming dependent on dictionaries and teachers. See the flow chart on the next page:

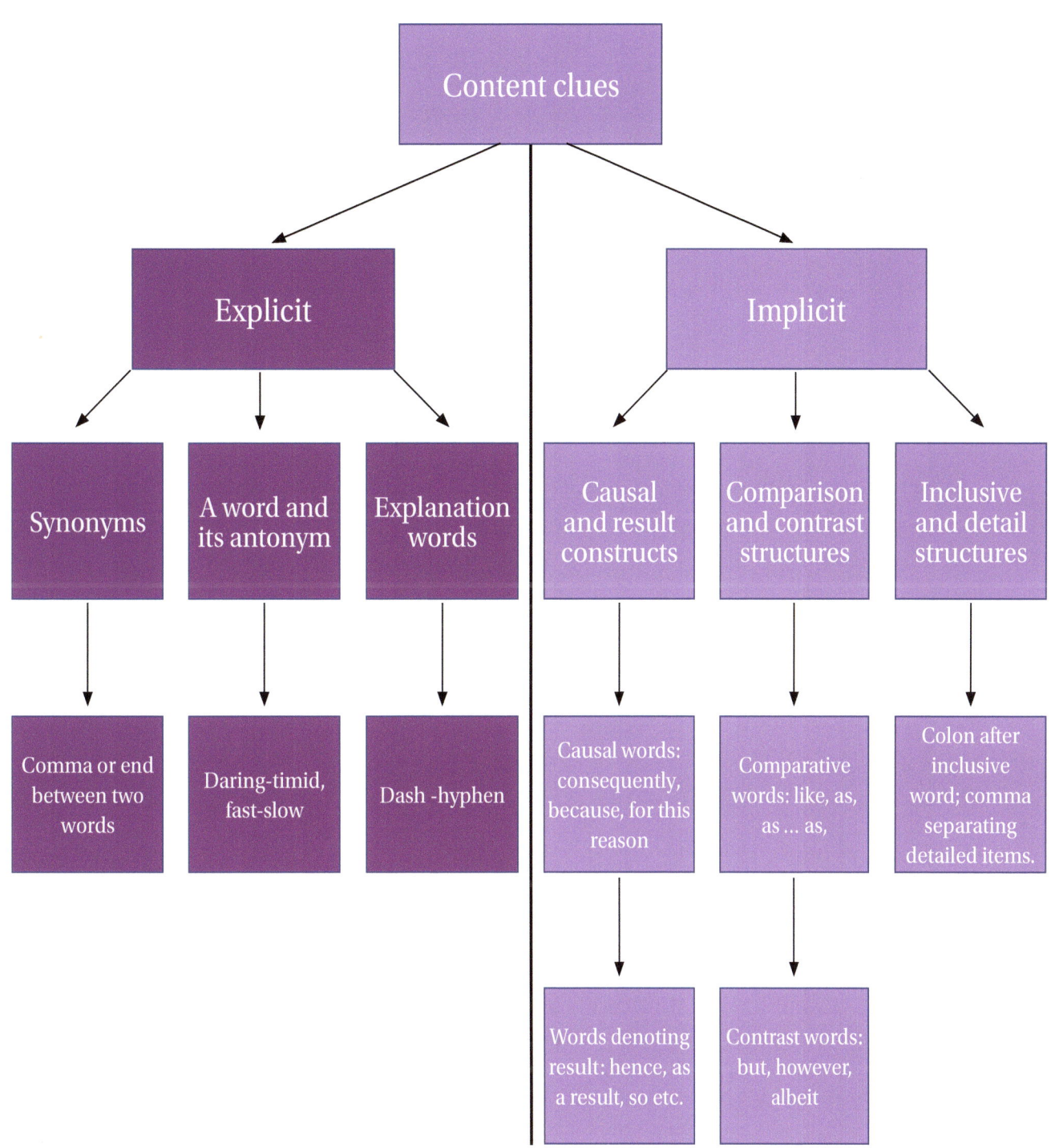

An Implicit Level of Interpretation

a. **Foretelling of Events**—this skill offers a reader the practice of reading between the lines. The reading goes beyond the written text and projects and foretells what will come next. By basing one's projections on logical thinking, this skill suggests a type of reading that will actively search for objectives while reading and will lead learners to establish some hypotheses about the text and then to test them.

Although this skill can lead to the establishment of some correct hypotheses, the result will be prescribed by the information of the text.

b. **Locating an Implicit Unstated Main Idea of a Text**—this skill develops in a reader the expertise of finding an idea not stated that can be traced by reading between the lines; namely by reading the text and locating the main ideas that are either predictable or interpretable.

First and foremost this skill is based on finding the main idea of a text while using an immediate verbal understanding.

Next, a reader is called upon to render an interpretation and give some thought in order to locate an unstated main idea.

c. **Drawing Conclusions**—the skill of drawing conclusions is an outcome of the implicit unstated main idea of a text. To achieve this skill a reader must render inductive and deductive thinking that can lead them to draw conclusions. Next, by basing the accumulation of interpreted sentences of a text, a reader can "justify" or reason the conclusions that were reached about the text.

d. **Identifying the Author's Viewpoint**—by using this skill a student identifies an author's personal implied viewpoint and/or attitude, when it is not explicitly stated in the text.

This skill is achievable through instructing a reader to look for clues that would showcase an author's viewpoint and ground them by citing phrases from the text.

e. **Reading the Protagonist's Feelings and Analyzing Characters**—this skill is achievable by developing a reader's sensitivity to be able to pinpoint a character or protagonist's personal feelings and characteristics and by instructing them to base their insights on the traceable physical portrayal and responses of characters.

Furthermore, classifying sentence tables that portray each character, a tool that was formerly demonstrated in a more primordial verbal comprehension phase, can also be found to be helpful for portraying characters.

f. **Linguistic Enrichment**—this skill consists of three above-mentioned linguistic enrichment tools and the building up of graded language. It is part and parcel of the literary subject that is simultaneously being taught.

Implemental Phase

In this phase a learner finally integrates skills that were acquired through the verbal and interpretive reading levels. In the implemental phase, the student can begin to link problem solving and implementation from within texts to application of these skills in real life situations.

Another skill suggested by this phase is critical reading of texts and assessing their correctness. Critical reading of a text is not achievable until a reader has used his or her verbal and interpretive reading skills for comprehending the author's main ideas. By doing so they can answer questions, a skill that is based on abstract thinking. However, in many cases the text offers some equally probable and acceptable answers to a specific question. The implementation level consists of the following skills:

a. **Problem Solving**

This skill is developed when reading material is the source for problem solving abilities eventually applied to the problems of daily life. This skill is equally accessible for any age of the reader. An equally important fact is that for each problem there are several equally acceptable solutions.

b. Critical Reading

Critical reading of a text is a more advanced cognitive skill than the implemental level or critical thinking. It involves the assessment and judgment of the text based on either a reader's own experience or on learned information.

While using the skill of critical reading a reader assesses the level of persuasiveness of a text at three different levels:

1. The level of its accuracy.
2. Distinguishing between opinions and facts.
3. Identifying literary/ literariness material.

Level of Text Accuracy

This skill involves exercising judgment and assessment over the level of literary or scientific accuracy of material learned by the student. This entails pointing out inaccuracies, stale or provocative facts, or out-of-date, inaccurate or irrelevant content.

Distinguishing Between Opinions and Facts

This skill involves the ability to distinguish between opinions and facts of a text, which is quite a complicated skill because sometimes opinions and facts are inseparably interwoven. Thus a reader might learn that a fact based on a valid fact is stronger than a baseless opinion.

Identifying Literary Material

This skill can help students distinguish between various literary genres e.g. prose, folktales, fables, scientific papers, propaganda etc. and to identify provocative sentences and announcements that are intended to persuade and make people change their minds, namely political articles. This is how students may learn about different methods of propaganda.

In Conclusion

The *Between the Lines* program practices the three levels of text understanding: its verbal, interpretive and implementation levels while foregrounding its linguistic program as an inseparable part of them. Some of the program texts exercise all three levels of thinking and skills. Others may only partially apply the set of understanding levels and skills. Hence, teachers are advised to add more skills to this triad of understanding levels and to use skills that match their class level and fit variances among the students.

The workbook icons:

 Verbal Understanding    Linguistic Understanding

 Interpretative Understanding    Implementation

 An explanation for students about the workbook's various learning skills.

 An explanation for both teachers and students about the workbook's various activities: oral and writing skills, listening, acting, painting and comics.

The Maid

A quarrel once arose between Reb Zev's wife and her maid. The mistress accused her of breaking a certain vessel and demanded that she compensate her for the damage. The maid denied guilt and refused to pay. The quarrel continued until she decided to summon the maid to a *din Torah* (judgment of a rabbinical court). Reb Zev saw that she was changing her clothes and going to see the rabbi, so he also put on his Shabbat clothes.

His wife asked why he was doing that. Reb Zev replied that he also wanted to go to see the rabbi.

His wife raised an objection to that and said that it was beneath his dignity since she herself would be able to plead properly in the rabbinical court.

"As for yourself, I have no doubt you will be able to do so," the tzadik (righteous man) replied, "but that poor orphan, the servant girl of yours, will not be able to plead properly and I want to speak for her because she has no one to plead her cause."

Based on a book published by the World Zionist Organization *"Leket from the Treasure House of Hasidim"* by Martin Buber, ed.: David Harden, 1969

Literal Understanding

What do sequential abilities mean?
This skill deals with understanding the events of the narrative according to its sequential order of sections, sentences and words that create the entire narrative.
This skill can be exercised by analyzing the sequences of segments, key sentences and keywords and by naming its segments according to their sequence.

1. Development of Sequential Abilities

a. Read the story attentively.

b. Check the keywords in each sentence.

What is a keyword?
Without keywords, a sentence might be meaningless.
To locate these words, one must raise the following two questions:
a. To whom does the sentence refer?
b. What does the sentence refer to?

c. Copy the sequence of the keywords you have checked, one by one:

Keywords:
_____
_____
_____

d. Summarize the tale by using the keywords.
Add conjunctions to the keywords.
_____
_____
_____
_____

B. Locating Details

Who said this to whom?

1. He also wanted to go to see the Rabbi. _____

2. "You will be able to do so." _____

3. "...that it was beneath his dignity..." _____

Find an alternative word:

1. Did not want to _____

2. This is inappropriate _____

3. A conflict started between Reb Zev's wife and her maid. _____

Classifications

Classify the keywords into the table below:

Reb Zev's wife	The maid	Reb Zev

C. Locating the Main Idea

What does the skill of locating the main idea mean?
The meaning of locating the main idea in a sentence/s is finding sentences that hold the most important idea of the text. To exercise this skill we must locate most of the keywords in the sentences.

1. The sentence below holds the main idea of the tale:

"You will be able to do so," the tzadik replied, "but that poor orphan, the servant girl of yours, will not be able to plead properly and I want to speak for her because she has no one to plead her cause."

a. Explain why this sentence holds the main idea.

_____

_____

_____

b. Write down how many keywords you found in this sentence and circle them.

_____

_____

 D. Language Enrichment

1. Classify the keywords in the table below:

Noun	Verb	Adjective

Causal Clauses—what does this mean?
Causal clauses can be classified into three types: fact, causal words, causality. Causal words can include conjunctions such as: *as, since, thus, for, hence.*

2. Compose three causal clauses that refer to content of the tale by using the words: as, since and hence.

(as...)_____
_____
_____

(since...)_____
_____
_____

(hence...)_____
_____
_____

3. In the tale, locate five combinations of the VERB-PREPOSITION-ARTICLE structure: For example: she **compensated** her **for the** damage.

_____
_____
_____
_____

Content cues—what do they mean?
There are two types of content cues: explicit and implicit.
Explicit content cues consist of three types: synonyms, a word and its antonym and an explanation.
Implicit content cues consist of causal cues, result constructs, negative clauses, comparative clauses and a whole and its part.

4. Identify the content cues of the following sentences. Circle the cue and classify it.

a. "but that poor orphan, the servant girl of yours, will not be able to plead properly"

b. "You will be able to do so (…) will not be able to plead"

c. "and I want to speak for her because she has no one to plead her cause."

Interpretive Comprehension

Locating a Main Idea That Is Not Stated Explicitly

What does an implicit main idea mean?
This skill involves identifying a main idea that is not stated explicitly in the text, and it can be practiced by raising questions. The main idea of a text is manifested in the sentence with the majority of keywords.

a. Reread the sentence containing the main idea in section C-1.

b. Classify Reb Zev and his wife's characteristics in the table below:

Reb Zev	Reb Zev's wife

c. Describe Reb Zev's behavior toward the maid.

_____

_____

_____

d. Describe Reb Zev's behavior toward his wife.

🍂 Implementation

a. Would you behave in the same way that Reb Zev did? Please explain.

b. In which other ways could the maid's problem be solved?

c. Can you give further examples in which a husband's opinion may differ to his wife's? Describe.

Students will orally identify or locate dominant characteristics of the tale and will refer to the following elements: exposition, the background of the tale, the characters and the narrative including its trigger event, its climax, resolution and conclusion.

The Sparrow

One day, upon returning from a hunting trip in the fields, I paced along a path in the park, my dog scampering ahead, until he suddenly halted and started to crawl quietly, as if he was sensing some sort of a hunt.

I stared toward the lane and observed a young sparrow that had fallen from its nest because of the fierce wind that toppled it onto the path from a birch tree. There it sat motionlessly, desperately spreading its budding wings.

My dog approached it stealthily, then all of a sudden an older sparrow flew up from over the treetop, and fell like a stone upon the dog's face. Then she rebounded twice, all ruffled and perplexed, chirping desperately and entreatingly in the face of the all-toothed jagged maw. She attacked in order to rescue; with her body enclosing her nestling… but its entire tiny body was shaking with fear, her chirp wild and broken, resembling a dead being—she sacrificed herself.

Couldn't the mother-bird perceive that the dog was an enormous, terrible animal? Despite the potential danger, she could not remain sitting soundly on her lofty and secure branch—a surge of power she could not contain dropped her down. My dog recoiled—probably he was also familiar with that kind of feeling power. I hurriedly called my perplexed dog, and we left that place of raw strength. I beg you, do not laugh: I was filled with awe, from the face of that tiny bird, from her brave spirit and gushing love that revealed itself at that moment.

Verbal Understanding

1. Development of sequential abilities

a. Read the story attentively.

b. Divide it into five segments of meanings.

c. Give a name to each of the segments.

1. _____

2. _____

3. _____

4. _____

5. _____

Locate five main key sentences in each of the segments.

1. _____

2. _____

3. _____

4. _____

5. _____

 ## 2. The Skill of Locating Details

What does the skill of locating details mean?

The skill of locating details deals with the minute details of the story and is practiced by:
1. Who said this to whom?
2. Find an alternative word.
3. True or false?
4. Classification tables

Answer the questions:

A. Portray the behavior of the dog upon returning from the hunting field.

_____

_____

_____

B. What caused the older sparrow to fall like a stone from the tree?

_____

_____

_____

C. Who saved the young sparrow?

_____

_____

_____

3. Mapping Out of Concepts

The skill of Classification tables

What does the skill of mapping out of concepts means?
Practicing the skill of mapping out of concepts endows the written story with a format of a graphical map of keywords that are embedded in this map. This skill is practiced by using flow charts, Venn Diagrams and Diffuse Mapping.

A. Reread the story.

B. With the following Venn Diagrams, you can understand the similarities and differences of each text (union and intersection).

C. The keyword kit on the following page persists of some of the keywords. Classify each keyword according to three of the story's characters and present more keywords.

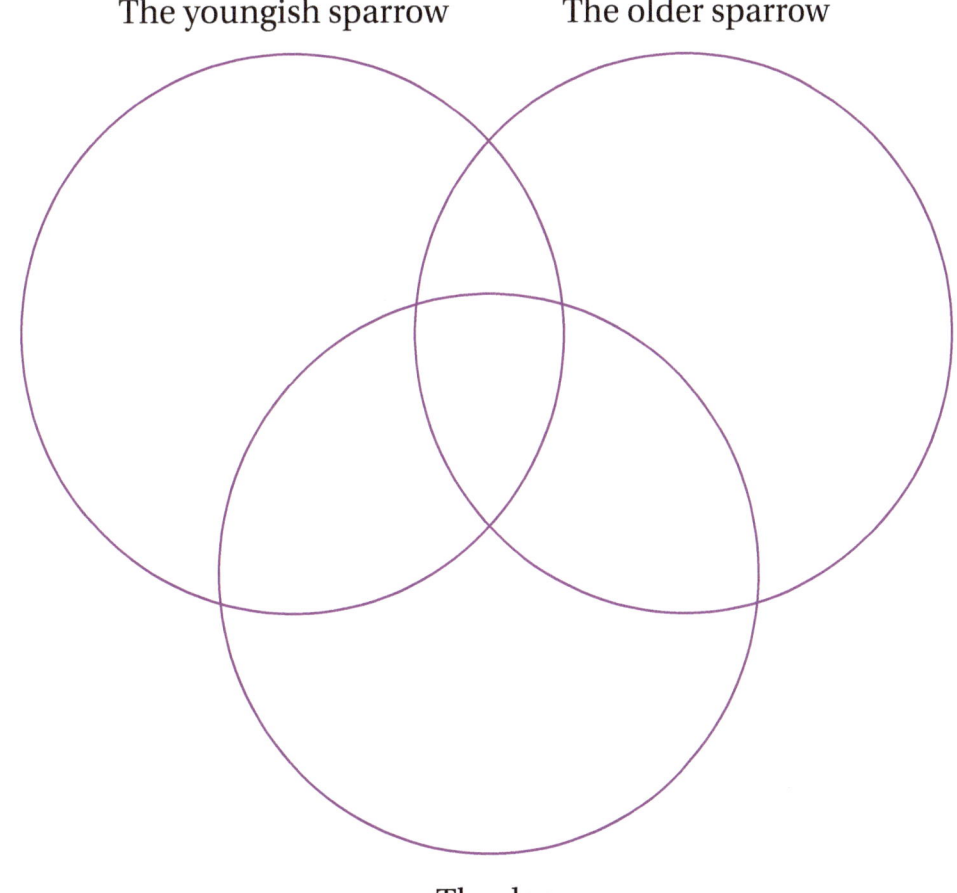

Keyword kit:

A youngish sparrow-dropped from its nest	an older sparrow flew up
Desperately spreading its wings	chirping desperately and entreatingly
My dog approached	Attacked for rescuing
With her body enclosing	Entire body shaking with fear
The dog was perceived like a terrible animal	An immense power dropped her down by her own accord
My dog was familiar with that power	

D. The following keywords contain some of the author's words. Add more keywords of your own.

- I paced along the path in the park
- I stared
- I hurriedly called my dog
- We left that place
- with awe
- from the face of her brave spirit
- and love of the small bird

E. Embed these keywords within the UNION section (the similarities) of the three circles.

F. Refer in your answer to the union section of the three circles.

1. What is the function of the union section of the circles? _____

2. What can we learn from this union? _____

G. Sum up the entire story by using the classified keyword that you imbedded in the circles. Add conjunctions.

_____
_____
_____
_____
_____
_____

H. Classify the following keyword kit according to the table on the following page:

Author	Young sparrow	Older sparrow	Dog

Keyword Kit:
Terrible animal, upon returning from hunting, enclosing with her body, an immense power, knocked down, awe, desperately spreading its wings, chirping desperately, offered herself as sacrifice, approached stealthily, hounded quietly, she attacked, he was also familiar with that power.

I. Add more words that portray the four characters in the above table.

Linguistic Enrichment

 **1. Word meanings**

Check the correct meaning of the word according to its textual context and circle it.

| A. sensing |

1. sneaked   2. ran away   3. fled away   4. felt

| B. quietly |

1. the opposite   2. boisterously   3. silently   4. forcefully

| C. youngish |

1. Antonym of harshly   2. All feathered   3. somewhat young   4. somewhat fat

| D. fierce |

1. to pierce   2. intensive   3. a feeling   4. hate

| E. enclosing |

1. covered   2. combed   3. hopped   4. hid herself

42

2. Implicit Content Cues

In implicit content cues you can find negative and comparative clauses. Comparative clauses are identifiable by words such as **like, as, likewise.** Negative clauses are identifiable by words such as **but, however.** Causal clauses can be identified by causal words such as **because**, **since**, **as**, **for**, **therefore** etc.

A. Copy four comparative clauses from the story.

_____

_____

_____

B. Copy one negative clause from the story.

_____

_____

_____

Interpretive Understanding

1. Locating a main idea

A. Locate the sentence with the main idea of the story and copy it.

B. Raise questions about a sentence with the main idea of the story by using the following WH-words:

How? Why? Whether? In which way? How come?

1. How? _____

_____

2. Why? _____

_____

3. Whether? _____

_____

4. How come? _____

_____

5. In which way? _____

_____

C. Give answers to the questions you have raised.

4. _____

_____

5. _____

_____

6. _____

_____

7. _____

_____

8. _____

_____

D. Which conclusion can you draw from those answers?

2. Analysis of Characters

What does analysis of characters mean?
This skill deals with drawing conclusions about the personal traits and feelings of the main characters of the story and is practiced by classification tables that focus on comparing characteristics, feelings, deeds etc.

A. Refer to the Classification Table on page 41 and write what kind of feelings the classified words awoke in you.

B. What can you learn about the main traits of the characters from the list of words you have classified in the table on page 41?

 # Implementation

A. State if you agree that it is possible that only mothers would risk their lives in order to save their children?

_____
_____
_____
_____

B. Are you aware of any other example of sacrificing one's life in order to rescue other people? (Among friends, warriors etc.)

_____
_____
_____
_____

C. Can you suggest any alternative way to rescue the nestling?

_____
_____
_____
_____

> Students will stage the story by casting the various characters and preparing the appropriate props.
> Students will rewrite the staging of the story while paying attention to the various stylistic changes that occur by moving from written language to verbal language.

The Three Counsels of the Rooster

A Jewish folktale from Poland

One day John Doe saw a rooster pecking on the pane of his window. He opened the window and caught it. Shortly afterward he realized its legs were tied with a band. The rooster opened its beak and began to speak, "If you would unleash my legs and set me free, I will give you three helpful tips."

"And what are they?" asked the man.

"First of all," replied the rooster, "swear to me that you are really going to let me go."

And the man made an oath to him.

The rooster said, "The first tip is about unbelievable things—don't believe in them!

The second tip is about something you cannot bring back—don't even think about it!

The third tip is about things that are above your capability—don't do them!"

As soon as the man set the rooster free, the latter jumped on a branch of a tree and exclaimed laughingly, "Woe to you, Man; you are such a gullible fool. I have in my throat a diamond treasure, and you set me free."

Bashfully regretting his own stupidity, the man rushed to get a grip on the rooster that hurried to jump higher. While climbing after him on the tree one of the boughs broke beneath him, and John Doe found himself on the ground, all bruised.

"A dupable fool!" laughed the rooster. "It has not yet been ten minutes since hearing my tips and you have already forgotten them all. You believed an unbelievable thing—can a diamond treasure be stored in a cockerel's throat? You felt regret for freeing me, and then tried to climb on boughs that were toppled by the weight of a rooster."

Raising Questions and Classifying Them

What does the skill of raising questions mean?
This skill deals with raising questions on three levels of thinking: verbal, interpretive and implemental. To practice this skill, use WH-words such as who, what, how much, where, whence, why, whether as well as what did they feel? What is your opinion? What would you do if …? etc.

A. Read the story *The Rooster's Three Tips* on the previous page.

B. Read the following twelve questions attentively:

1. What was the rooster doing on John Doe's window?
2. What would you do if you were John Doe after finding out that you were cheated?
3. What did John Doe do to the rooster after he pecked on his window?
4. Why, in your opinion, did the rooster counsel John Doe not to believe in unbelievable things?
5. Why did the rooster counsel John Doe?
6. Where did John Doe catch the rooster?
7. When did John Doe discover that the rooster had cheated him?
8. Why, in your opinion, did the rooster counsel John Doe never to think about something he cannot bring back?
9. Why, in your opinion, did John Doe catch the rooster?
10. How, in your opinion, did the rooster feel after being caught?
11. Was John Doe right about trying to catch the rooster again?
12. What were the rooster's tips?

C. Refer to the twelve questions above:

　　Circle WH-words that concern **verbal understanding** in **green**.

　　Circle questions that concern **interpretive understanding** in **red**.

　　Circle **implementation questions** in **blue**.

D. Classify the twelve questions above according to the following table:

An answer exists in the story	An answer does not exist in the story

E. Classify the twelve questions on the previous page according to the following three categories (that hold generalizing titles):

Questions concerning John Doe	Questions concerning the rooster	Questions concerning the rooster's tips

F. Classify the previous twelve questions according to the following three categories (that hold generalizing titles):

Identification	Judgments and criticism	Feelings

G. Compose twelve additional questions according to the text of *The Rooster's Three Tips*:

1. _____
2. _____
3. _____
4. _____
5. _____
6. _____
7. _____
8. _____
9. _____
10. _____
11. _____
12. _____

 **Mapping of Concepts: Venn Diagrams**

A. Use the following three Venn circles to embed more keywords and key sentences in each circle according to the generalized titles in Tables E and F:

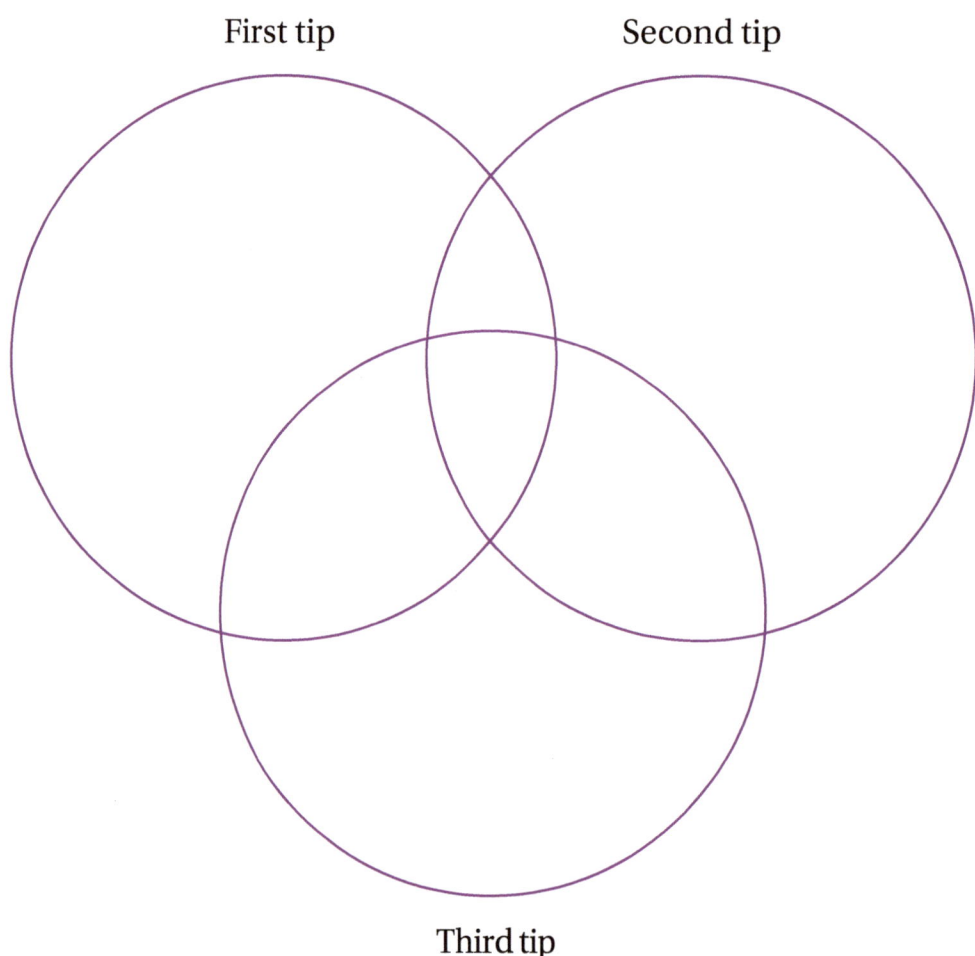

What is a keyword?

Keywords are the main words in a sentence. Without keywords the sentence might become meaningless.

To locate these words, one must raise the following two questions:

a. To whom does the sentence refer?

b. What does the key sentence refer to?

What does a key sentence mean?
A key sentence is the most significant sentence in a paragraph. Without it the paragraph becomes meaningless.

B. Embed in the following Venn circles keywords and key sentences:

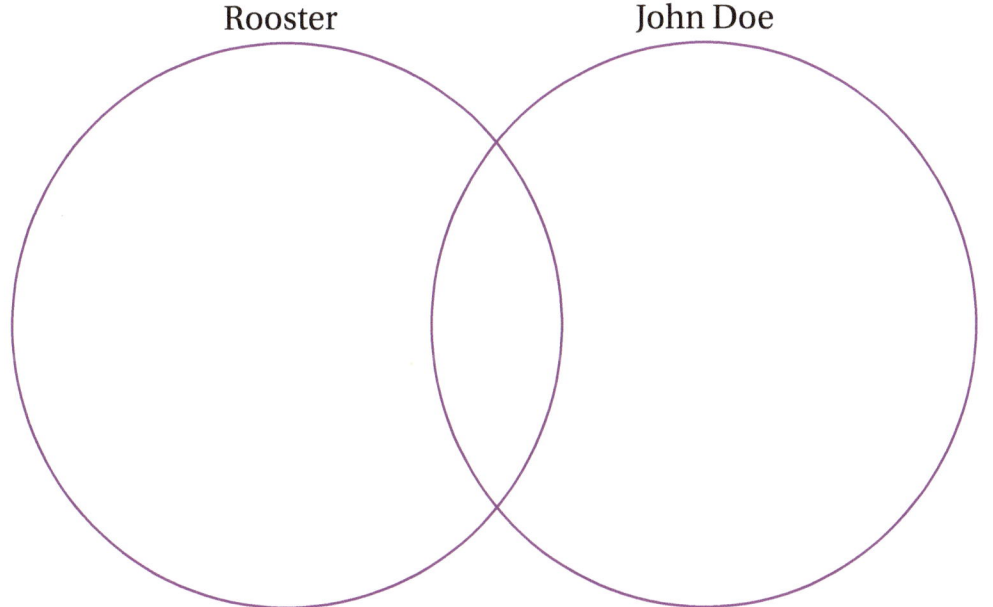

C. What is common to all the three Venn circles? _____

D. What is common to the two Venn circles? _____

Interpretive Understanding

Locating Not-Stated Main Ideas: Drawing Conclusions

What does it mean to draw a conclusion?
This skill deals with conclusions and lessons to be learned from the text of the story. It is practiced by raising WH-word questions such as how, why, whether and in which way, which shall be targeting sentences that hold the main idea.

A. Identify the sentence with the main idea.

B. What helped you identify the main idea?

C. Circle all the keywords in the sentence.

D. Raise questions that hold the main idea and can help in drawing conclusions. Use the following WH-words:

Why? _____

_____

How? _____

_____

Whether? _____

_____

which? _____

_____

E. Compose two sentences for each category in the following table:

Causal clauses	Result constructs	Comparative clauses
Causal words: *as, since, thus, for, hence*	Words denoting result: as, therefore, hence, as a result	Comparative words: *like, as, such that, such as*
1. _____	1. _____	1. _____
2. _____	2. _____	2. _____
3. _____	3. _____	3. _____
4. _____	4. _____	4. _____
5. _____	5. _____	5. _____

Contrast clauses	Enumerating and concluding clauses
Contrast words: *but, on one hand ….on the other hand; in contrast; contrastingly*	*Colon* after the enumerating word and *commas* after each of the listed details Example–Ofra had five pens: blue, green, yellow, orange and red.
1. _____	1. _____
2. _____	2. _____
3. _____	3. _____
4. _____	4. _____
5. _____	5. _____
6. _____	6. _____
7. _____	7. _____

Students will create comics; a verbal story based on a chronological sequence of cartooned frames. Speech and thoughts will be put into balloons, respectively.

Not to Shame
by I. L. Peretz

One time, when Rabbi Yechiel entered his home, he found a man standing in his room and stashing something under the flap of his coat. At the sight of Rabbi Yechiel, the man fainted with fear. He attempted to hide the protruding object under his clothes. Rabbi Yechiel, who was well acquainted with the man and knew he was not a thief, God forbid, but rather a poor and decent man who had come upon a difficult time and had come to ask for support, but was not able to resist the temptation.

With a warm welcome Rabbi Yechiel said to the man, "A moneylender you need, I see my friend. A pawn you have brought, have you? Please show me the pawn." The poor man stood there, his teeth chattering.

"And why are you ashamed, you good Jewish man? The wheel of fortune is turning around and around. Today I lend you; tomorrow you lend me. Do not feel shame."

At that moment, he approached the man, pulled out a silver lantern from under the man's garment and laid it down on the table. Rabbi Yechiel behaved as if he were seeing the lantern for the first time, examining it with an expert eye, while his companion was waiting with bated breath, wanting to run away but unable to move his legs, as if they were chained.

"And how much do you need, my good man?" asked Rabbi Yechiel.

But the man had lost his tongue, and was at a loss for words.

"I see you are the shyest of men on earth, my good Jewish man. Ay… well… well… but… What can be done? I'll try to be a mouth for you."

"Indeed," said Rabbi Yechiel, "the high holidays are impending, and I doubt if you have enough to put food on the family table during the high holidays. I beg you, are you in need of anything?"

And the poor man just lowered his head.

"Certainly! I'm not a prophet or a son of a prophet, but surely your face betrays you—and perhaps you have another daughter that ought to be married?"

The miserable man could not hold his tears anymore and started to weep full-heartedly.

"And why are you weeping? Don't be a fool, because I already told you; the wheel of fortune is turning around and around… and even so… my good Jewish rebbe, you are not allowed to weep this way in front of me. By law I'm obliged to lend you at a time of hardship, and not listen to the sound of your weeping. And since you are not intending to pronounce how much you need, I shall lend you according to the pawn. At first glance of an expert eye I can tell you that the value of this pawn is equivalent to at least one hundred shekels, so I shall lend you at least seventy; ten for holiday supplies; fifty as a dowry and another ten for the wedding. And when you come into some money – you will pay me back.

The man stood there, his entire body trembling; unable to reach out for the money in Rabbi Yechiel's palm.

Rabbi Yechiel put the money into the pocket of the poor man and asked him to hurry back home to get prepared with supplies for the holiday. "Time is short," he said, "and there are many supplies to get, my friend."

The following story has been divided into segments of meaning:

Not to Shame by I. L. Peretz

One time when Rabbi Yechiel entered his home, he found a man standing in his room and stashing something under the flap of his coat. At the sight of Rabbi Yechiel, the man fainted with fear. He attempted to hide the protruding object under his clothes. Rabbi Yechiel, who was well acquainted with the man and knew he was not a thief, God forbid, but rather a poor and decent man who had come upon a difficult time, had come to ask for support, but was not able to resist temptation.

With a warm welcome Rabbi Yechiel said to the man,
"A moneylender you need, I see my friend. A pawn you have brought, have you? Please show me the pawn." The poor man stood there, his teeth chattering.
"And why are you ashamed, you good Jewish man? The wheel of fortune is turning around and around. Today I lend you; tomorrow you lend me. Do not feel shame."

At that moment, he approached the man, pulled out a silver lantern from under the man's garment and laid it down on the table. Rabbi Yechiel behaved as if he was seeing the lantern for the first time, examining it with an expert eye, while his companion was waiting with bated breath, wanting to run away but unable to move his legs, as if they were chained.

"And how much do you need, my good man?" asked Rabbi Yechiel.
But the man had lost his tongue, and was at a loss for words.
"I see you are the shyest of men on earth, my good Jewish man. Ay… well… well… but…What can be done? I'll try to be a mouth for you."
"Indeed," said Rabbi Yechiel, "the high holidays are impending, and I doubt if you have enough to put food on the family table during the high holidays. I beg you, are you in need of anything?"
And the poor man just lowered his head.
"Certainly! I'm not a prophet or a son of a prophet but surely your face betrays you—and perhaps you have another daughter that ought to be married?"

The miserable man could not hold his tears anymore and started to weep full-heartedly. "And why are you weeping? Don't be a fool because I already told you; the wheel of fortune is turning around and around…and even so… my good Jewish rebbe, you are not allowed to weep this way in front of me. By law I'm obliged to lend you at a time of hardship, and not listen to the sound of your weeping.

And since you are not intending to pronounce how much you need, I shall lend you according to the pawn. At first glance of an expert eye I can tell you that the value of this pawn is equivalent to at least one hundred shekels, so thus I shall lend you at least seventy; ten for holiday supplies; fifty as a dowry and another ten for the wedding. And when you come into some money, you will pay me back.

The man stood there, his entire body trembling; unable to reach out for the money in Rabbi Yechiel's palm.

Rabbi Yechiel put the money into the pocket of the poor man and asked him to hurry back home to get prepared with supplies for the holiday. "Time is short," he said, "and there are many supplies to get, my friend."

# Verbal Understanding

A. Read the story *Not to Shame* by I. L. Peretz.

B. On the previous pages the book has been divided into paragraphs of meaning.

C. Give a name to each segment. Use the empty lines below:

D. Locate a key sentence in each segment and write it below:

E. Locate keywords in the key sentences you have written down and circle them.

F. Add conjunctions.

G. Summarize the story.

_____

_____

_____

_____

1. Raising and classifying of questions:

B. Read the story.

C. Compose twelve questions about the story.

1. _____

2. _____

3. _____

4. _____

5. _____

6. _____

7. _____

8. _____

9. _____

10. _____

11. _____

12. _____

C. Classify the questions you've composed in the following table:

An answer exists in the story	An answer does not exist in the story

D. Classify the questions you composed according to the titles of the table below:

Questions concerning the poor man	Questions concerning Rabbi Yechiel	Questions concerning charity and benevolence

E. Classify the questions you composed in the table below:

Emotions	Judgments and criticism	Identification

2. Classification of Concepts

A. Read the story *Not to Shame* by the author I. L. Peretz.

B. On page 66 there is a flow chart.

C. On page 67 there are some keywords and key sentences.

D. Locate more keywords and key sentences and embed them correctly according to their right order in the empty frames of the flow chart.

E. Sum up the story in the following lines:

_____

_____

_____

Flow Chart

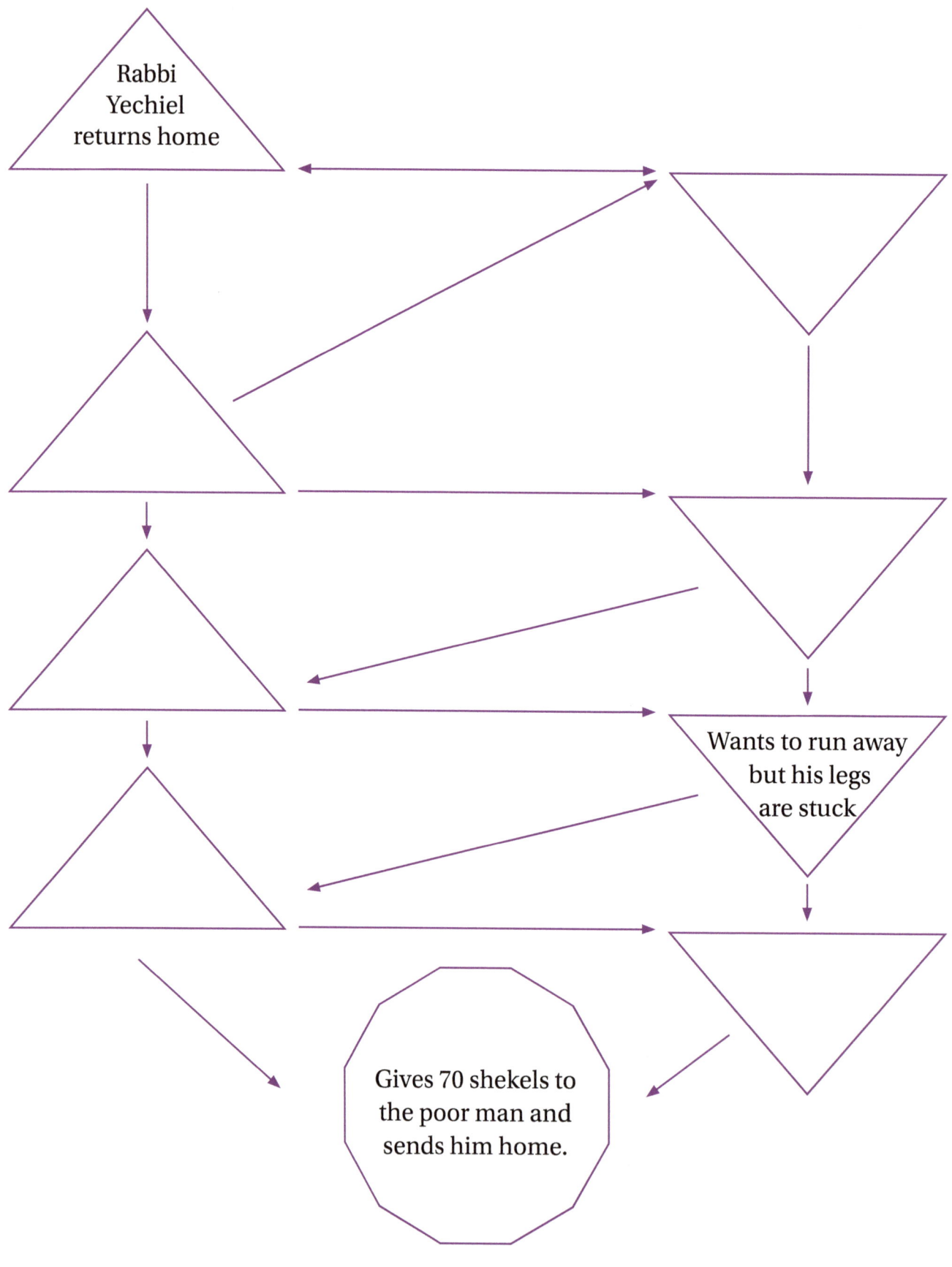

Embed the keywords and key sentences of this page in the flow chart of the previous page.

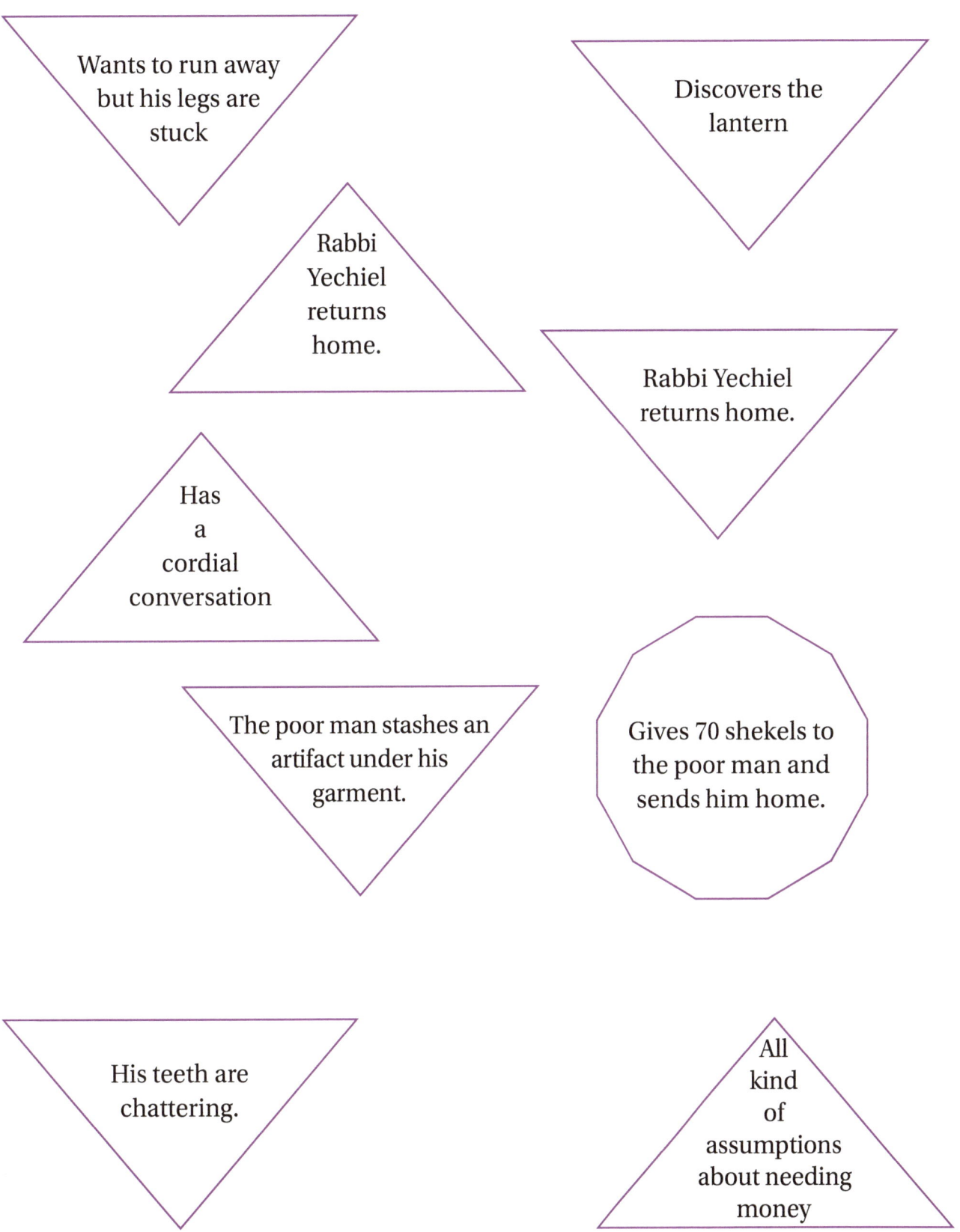

Linguistic Enrichment

A. Reread *Not to Shame* by I. L. Peretz.

B. The following mixed sentences in the frames are made up from causal words, causal clauses and factual sentences.

C. Classify them accordingly in the table below:

Fact	Causal words	Causality

The poor man took the lantern.	Not to shame the poor man	He didn't want Rabbi Yechiel to realize what he had taken.
And embarrassedly felt shame about his deeds	since for	He could not resist the temptation.
Rabbi Yechiel pretended that he didn't see it.	because	The poor man didn't answer Rabbi Yechiel.
	Rabbi Yechiel put the money in the poor man's pocket.	The poor man stashed the lantern.

D. Compose six result constructs that refer to the story.

E. Circle words that express results (as a result, therefore, hence) in **red.**

F. Circle sentences that denote facts in **green**.

G. Circle sentences that denote results in **blue**.

_____
_____
_____
_____
_____
_____
_____

 Students will write an article based on the story using a journalistic tone and will integrate photographs of the "event."

Small Fish, Big Fish

A Jewish folktale from Poland. Recorded by Gershon Brivrav and told by Arie Tesler.

The head of one congregation was a well known miser. All the local beggars knew about it and made it known to all.

One day, a great honor befell the head of the community: a great and famous *tzadik* honored him by paying a visit to his home. No choice was left for the head of the congregation but to ask the *tzadik* to stay for lunch.

The head of the congregation consulted with his wife, who was a bigger miser than he, and both chose to include fish on the menu.

At lunch they would serve some small fish, while the big ones would be kept for dinner so they could savor them all by themselves, after the *tzadik* left. However, the *tzadik* already happened to see the simmering food on the kitchen stove and he could almost feel the splendid taste of the cooking fish on his tongue. His disappointment was very deep when he realized that only small fish were served on his plate. He bent over the dish, and it seemed as if he was whispering and conversing with the fish. The shocked couple sat and quietly watched the revelation of an immense miracle: a tremendous miracle occurred in their home, and they could see with their own eyes a *tzadik* conversing with fish. Indeed, the story of the great miracle that happened in their home would be retold and passed on to generations to come.

Not long afterward, the head of the congregation daringly said to the *tzadik*, "Your honorable tzadik, may you live to be a hundred and twenty, do you sir comprehend the language of fish and can you speak with them?"

"Undoubtedly." said the rabbi with a sigh. "Since my brother drowned in the river, I used to ask the fish if they had happened to meet him. They replied, 'when the tragedy happened we hadn't been born yet, but there are some big fish in the kitchen: they would probably know the answer.'"

 **Verbal Understanding**

1. The story below is divided into four segments of meaning:

> **A.** The head of one congregation was a tremendous miser and everyone knew about it. All the local beggars knew about it and made it known to all.

> **B.** One day a great honor befell the head of the community: a great and famous *tzadik* honored him by paying a visit to his house. No choice was left for the head of the congregation but to ask the *tzadik* to stay for lunch.
> The head of the congregation consulted with his wife, who was a bigger miser than he, and both chose to include fish on the menu.
> At lunch they would serve some small fish, while the big ones would be kept for dinner so that they could savor them all by themselves, after the *tzadik* left.

> **C.** However, the *tzadik* already happened to see the simmering food on the kitchen stove and he could almost feel the splendid taste of the cooking fish on his tongue. His disappointment was very deep when he realized that only small fish were served on his plate. He bent over the dish, and it seemed as if he was whispering and conversing with the fish. The shocked couple sat and quietly watched the revelation of an immense miracle: a tremendous miracle occurred in their home, and they could see with their own eyes a *tzadik* conversing with fish. Indeed the story of the great miracle that happened in their home would be retold and passed on to generations to come.

> **D.** Not long afterward, the head of the congregation daringly said to the tzadik, "Your honorable *tzadik*, may you live to be a hundred and twenty, do you sir comprehend the language of fish and can you speak with them?"
> "Undoubtedly." said the rabbi with a sigh. "Since my brother drowned in the river, I used to ask the fish if they had happened to meet him. They replied, 'when the tragedy happened we hadn't been born yet, but there are some big fish in the kitchen: they would probably know the answer.'"

2. Pair the mixed-up titles below into the four segments of meaning above.

A. The menu that was prepared for the honorable guest

B. The guest's disappointment and his conversation with the fish

C. The *tzadik* confessed that he knew about the big fish in the kitchen in front of the head of the congregation.

D. The miser was head of the congregation.

3. The following key sentences became mixed up. Pair each one to the appropriate segment below:

> The head of the congregation and his wife decided that at lunch they would eat some small fish, while the big ones would be kept for dinner so that they could savor them all by themselves, after the tzadik left.

> One day, a great and famous *tzadik* honored him by visiting his home.

> Undoubtedly." said the rabbi with a sigh. "Since my brother drowned in the river, I used to ask the fish if they had happened to meet him.

> The *tzadik* threw a glance to the kitchen and he could almost feel the splendid taste of the fish. His disappointment was very deep when he realized that only small fish were served on his plate.

> He bent over the dish, and it seemed as if he was whispering and conversing with the fish.

> The head of that congregation was a tremendous miser and everyone knew about it.

> The head of the congregation asked, "Your honorable *tzadik*, do you comprehend the language of fish?"

> And they replied, 'When the tragedy happened we hadn't been born yet, but there are some big fish in the kitchen: they would probably know the answer.'"

Segment A. _____
_____

Segment B. _____
_____

Segment C. _____
_____

Segment D. _____
_____

4. Sum up the story by using the key words on page 77.

5. Locate the sentence with the main idea among these key sentences.

6. Explain in which way you located the sentence with the main idea.

What is a keyword?
Keywords are the main words in a sentence. Without keywords the sentence might become meaningless.
To locate these words one must raise the following two questions:
a. To whom does the sentence refer?
b. What does the key sentence refer to?

What does a key sentence mean?
A key sentence is the most significant sentence in a paragraph. Without it the paragraph becomes meaningless.

Use the keywords to summarize the story:

_____
_____

> **What does the skill of locating the main idea mean?**
> The meaning of locating the main idea in a sentence/s is finding sentences that hold the most important idea of the text. To exercise this skill we must locate most of the keywords in the sentences.

Write down the sentence with the main idea:

_____
_____
_____
_____
_____

In which way did you locate the sentence with the main idea?

_____
_____
_____
_____
_____

* The students will discuss the subject of being stingy – being a miser, while taking a personal side and exemplifying situations.
* The students will point to different types of humor and tell jokes on the subject of being stingy.

Here is a list of keywords:

Head of the congregation	Miser	The answer
Great *tzadik*	Honored	His visit
Chose	Menu	Small fish
Big	For themselves	Know
Peep at	Their taste	Of the fish
His disappointment	Realized	Small fish
Bent over	Conversing	With the fish
Presented	Can he comprehend the language of fish	
Undoubtedly	My brother	Drowned
Ask	To meet him	Big fish
When	Tragedy	We were not born yet

The Bundle of Sticks
by Aesop

One time an old man summoned his sons. "I'm close to death," he said, "but before my passing away I want to demonstrate to you some valuable tenets. Bring me some sticks."

The sons went out to the yard, gathered and brought him some sticks. The father gave each son one stick and asked them, "Please break the sticks." Each one of them, even the youngest, broke their stick effortlessly.

The father gathered the remaining sticks into one bundle. "Now try, when they are in a bunch." The oldest son tried unsuccessfully, and then the second son and the third and so on to the last one but the sticks would not break.

"Behold," said the father, "each one of you broke with ease a single feeble stick, but none of you managed to break the bundle of sticks. And you are the same—when each one of you is alone you are weak, but united no one can break you."

 **Verbal Understanding**

 **What does a deficient passage mean? (Cloze paragraphs).**
The skill of filling in a deficient passage enables a learner to replace missing words by relying on contextual cues. A student can base his or her filling in on their previous knowledge and textual context or by citing a word from the text.

1. Fill in the following deficient passage with the missing words:

One time an old man _____ his sons. "I'm close to death," he said, "but before my passing away I want to demonstrate to you some _____. Bring me some _____."

The sons went out to the yard, gathered and brought him some sticks. The father gave each son one stick and _____ them, "Please break the sticks." Each one of them, even the youngest, broke their stick _____.

The father gathered the remaining sticks into one _____. "Now try, when they are in a bunch." The oldest son tried _____, and then the second son and the third and so on to the last one but the sticks would not break.

"Behold," said the father, "each one of you broke with ease a _____ feeble stick, but none of you managed _____ the bundle of sticks. And you are the same—when each one of you is alone you are weak, but _____ no one can break you."

2. Copy the main-idea sentences from the tale.

_____
_____
_____

3. Locate in the main-idea sentences, keywords that give each sentence a meaning.

_____
_____
_____

4. Classify the words you filled in the deficient passages as nouns, verbs and adjectives:

Nouns	Verbs	Adjectives

5. Compose two causal clauses by using words such as *because, since, as, for, therefore,* which are related to the content of the story.

_____
_____
_____

Compose two sentences denoting results by using words like *as a result, therefore, hence,* which are related to the content of the story.

_____
_____
_____

6. Add synonyms or some explanations to the following words:

Sticks _____

Valuable _____

Bundle _____

Single _____

Remained _____

Interpretive Understanding

Main-Idea Sentences

A. Refer to the two main-idea sentences and by using the four following WH-words, raise questions about each sentence and then answer the questions you made.

Why? _____

_____

How? _____

_____

Whether? _____

_____

How come? _____

_____

B. What have you learned from the lesson that the father taught his sons?

_____

_____

_____

C. Which personal traits characterize the father?

_____

_____

_____

_____

 # Implementation

 **Problem Solving**

What does the skill of problem solving mean?
This skill can be helpful for learners as a tool for solving their own daily problems.
The skill could be practiced by asking questions like, 'What would you do instead?', 'Would you do the same as him?' or 'How did you feel?'

Do you consider the example given as the bundle of sticks a good example?

_____
_____
_____
_____
_____
_____
_____
_____
_____
_____

 * The students will tell about similar situations with the message that two are better than one.
* The students will use the dictionary to find Jewish phrases, idioms and proverbs that connote similar messages to the proverb two are better than one.

Alternative Assessment:
Indicator of Reading and Comprehension on Three Levels of Thinking

Student name: _____ Class: _____ School: _____ Level of implementation: _____

Literal understanding	Starting out	Progress achieving the goal	Achieving the goal
Sequence	Did not understand the meaning of the sequence and did not accomplish assignments that associate with sequence of segments, key sentences and keywords.	Partly understood sequential assignments and partly achieved them.	Understood the meaning of sequential narrative and accomplished all assignments associated with sequence of segments, key sentences and keywords.
Detail locating	Did not locate details of the following skills: "Who said that to whom?" "What was said instead?" Classifications.	Partly located skills of detail finding and classifications.	Fully located details in the following skills: Who said that to whom? What was said instead? Classifications.
Identifying the main idea	Did not identify the sentence that holds a wealth of keywords, which is the main-idea sentence.	Partly identified keywords but did not identify the main-idea sentence.	Identified key sentences that have keywords, which are main-idea sentences.
Mapping of concepts (flow charts, Diffuse Mapping, Venn Diagrams)	Did not embed keywords and key sentences correctly in the three types of mappings: flow charts, Venn Diagrams and Diffuse Mapping.	Partly embedded keywords and key sentences in the three types of mappings: flow charts, Venn Diagrams and Diffuse Mapping.	Embedded keywords correctly and key sentences correctly in the three types of mappings: flow charts, Venn Diagrams and Diffuse Mapping.

Alternative Assessment:
Indicator of Reading and Comprehension on Three Levels of Thinking

Student name: _____ Class: _____ School: _____ Level of implementation: _____

Literal understanding	Starting out	Progress achieving a goal	Achieving the goal
Dividing into segments of meaning	Did not divide text according to correct segments of meaning, and were not cognizant of naming each paragraph.	Divided the text into meaning segments but did not name them.	Divided the text correctly into segments of meaning, and named each segment appropriately.
Locating of key sentences	Did not locate key sentences by using WH-words such as: Who is the segment talking about? What is the segment talking about?	Partly located key sentences by raising questions that separate the wheat from the chaff.	Located key sentences by questions such as who is the segment talking about? What is the segment talking about.
Locating of keywords	Did not locate keywords and separate the wheat from the chaff by asking WH-questions such as: Who is the segment talking about? What is the segment talking about?	Partly located keywords in key sentences and partly separated the wheat from the chaff by asking WH-questions such as: Who is the segment talking about? What is the segment talking about?	Located key words in key sentences and separated the wheat from the chaff by raising these questions.
Raising and classifying of questions	Did not use all WH-words in all three levels of thinking and did not classify them according to different classifications (5 classification tables).	Partly used WH-words in all three levels of thinking and partly classified them according to different classifications (5 classification tables).	Used all WH-words in all three levels of thinking and classified them according to different classifications (5 classification tables).
Summarization skills	Did not implement summarization skills by using keywords, key sentences and conjunctions.	Partly implemented summarization skills by using keywords, key sentences and conjunctions.	Fully implemented summarization skills by using keywords, key sentences and conjunctions.
Language enrichment	Did not implement the various linguistic assignments.	Partly implemented the various linguistic assignments.	Fully implemented the various linguistic assignments.

Alternative Assessment:
Indicator of Reading and Comprehension on Three Levels of Thinking

Student name: _____ Class: _____ School: _____ Level of implementation: _____

Literal understanding	Starting out	Progress achieving the goal	Achieving the goal
Drawing conclusions	Did not know how to draw conclusions from the text and implement conclusion-related assignments. Did not know how to raise main-idea, interpretive-understanding questions.	Partly achieved the skill of drawing conclusions and partly implemented the interpretive understanding of main idea questions.	Could fully draw conclusions from the text and raise the correct questions about the main idea by using interpretive understanding.
Not-stated implicit main idea of the text	Did not know how to raise main-idea, interpretive-understanding questions and thus did not identify not-stated main idea.	Partly achieved the skill of raising questions and interpretive-understanding questions to identify not-stated main idea.	Fully achieved all skills needed for identifying not-stated main idea by using interpretive understanding questions.
Prediction of events	Did not know how to foretell the story's next event because of lack of understanding of its first part.	Partly knew to foretell the story's forthcoming events by leaning on the partial understanding of the story.	Full capacity of prediction forthcoming events of the story by relying on his/her understanding of the story.
Author's attitude	Did not know to identify the author's attitude by relying on the text and using interpretive understanding skills.	Partly identified the author's attitude through using interpretive understanding skills.	Fully understood author's attitude.

Alternative Assessment:
Indicator of Reading and Comprehension on Three Levels of Thinking

Student name: _____ Class: _____ School: _____ Level of implementation: _____

Literal understanding	Starting out	Progress achieving the goal	Achieving the goal
Distinguishing between fact and opinion	Did not identify the differences between facts and opinions and did not use identification skills for distinguishing between them.	Partly identified the differences between facts and opinions and partly used identification skills for distinguishing between them.	Identified the differences between facts and opinions and used good identification skills for distinguishing between them.
Form an Opinion	Did not know how to crystallize and formalize personal opinion while basing it on text.	Partly knew how to crystallize and formalize personal opinion while basing it on text.	Fully crystallized and formalized personal opinions that were an outcome of the text.
Solving of applied problems based on text	Could not apply his/her textual acquired knowledge to everyday life.	Could partly apply his/her textual acquired knowledge to everyday life.	Knew how to solve applied problems based on textual understanding and could accommodate it to student's everyday life.

Learning Journal

Student name: _____ Class: _____

School: _____ Level of implementation: _____

Alternative Assessments

1. What does sequence mean?

   _____
   _____
   _____

2. Why is a narrative sequence so important in the story?

   _____
   _____
   _____

3. What have you learned about your learning process during this activity?

   _____
   _____
   _____

4. Why is it important to locate key words and sentences in the text?

   _____
   _____
   _____

5. With which WH-words did you locate keywords in the key sentences?

_____

_____

_____

6. Which tools are there for locating a main idea?

_____

_____

_____

7. Did you have any difficulty with locating the main idea?

_____

_____

_____

8. What are raising and classifying questions important for?

_____

_____

_____

9. What did you learn about yourself during this activity?

_____

_____

_____

10. Why is it important to implement all the various phases of the assignment?

11. How would you be able to apply all the phases to other assignments as well?

12. Why do we need to locate textual details?

13. What is a flow chart and what it is used for?

14. Which skills did you use to build a flow chart?

15. You have been exposed to various types of mappings. When would you use each one of them?

16. Does the mapping system apply to your learning skills? If yes, explain why.

17. What have you learned about yourself through mapping?

18. Which kind of tools helped you draw your conclusions?

19. What kinds of clues belong to explicit content clues?

20. What types of clues belong to implicit content clues?

21. What can you learn from locating explicit and implicit content clues?

22. What do you think are the differences between the verbal, interpretive and implemental levels of understanding?

23. What did you find helpful and applicable for the assignments at the three levels of understanding?

24. Which of the three levels of thinking is more feasible to use?

25. Which of the three levels of thinking is more difficult to use?

26. How would you explain the notion of implemental level?

27. What is needed for completing the implemental level of assignments?

28. Which strategy would you change if you were to write it yourself?

29. Which type of skill did you like best and why?

Tables of Graded Language Patterns

Linguistic constructs	Samples	Important notes
Phase A: 1. Linguistic patterns Simple sentence– Nominal clause	* a yellow flower. * a table.	Nominal clauses are quite rare in English when the copula *be is omitted.
2. Simple sentence–verbal clause	* Uri stud**ies**. * Hanna sits.	It is recommended to begin with present simple and then move to past simple and present perfect.
3. Simple sentence + temporal clause	* Ronny studies **in the mornings.**	Temporal clauses are time complements that denote time like morning, afternoon, night, etc.
4. Simple sentence + locative clause	* The book is **on the table.**	Usually this linguistic construct consists of the sequence *verb + preposition. Prepositions are particles like on, under, off, next to, behind–words that could not be in plural voice.
5. Simple interrogative questions	* **Who** ate the cream? * **How** many pages are in the book? * **Where** do you live?	WH interrogatives can be identified by their WH-words such as why, where, who, when, whom, whether, etc.
6. Object clause	* I bought **the book.**	Usually an object clause will come after the verb and sometimes it is preceded by delimitative ***the.**
7. Possessive clause	* I **have** the book. * I **don't have** the book.	Usually these are marked by the word *have.

Tables of Graded Language Patterns

Linguistic constructs	Samples	Important notes
8. Auxiliary verbs + verbs Can, could, shall, should, will, would, may, might, have, had, etc.	* I **must learn** Hebrew. * I **can learn** Hebrew.	Auxiliary verbs (or help-words) provide an emotive force to the sentence and verbs in this construct will stay uninflected. They should be taught after teaching simple past and present.
9. Causal clause	* We did not go on the trip **because** it was raining. * We went to eat **since** we were hungry.	Causal clauses may be identified by causal words such as **because, since, as, for, therefore,** etc., which usually head an independent clause. However, their position might be at the beginning or end of sentence.
10. Result constructs	* The ox could tolerate no more of this work, **so** he asked the man.	Using conjunctions like *as a result, therefore, so, hence* that denote the construct of result.
11. Comparative clause	* Ronny plods **like** a turtle.	Through using comparative words such as **like, as, such that, such as,** etc., two facts are being compared to each other. Usually, a comparative clause will come at the end of sentence.

Tables of Graded Language Patterns

Linguistic constructs	Samples	Important notes
12. Contrast clause but, on one hand…., on the other hand, in contrast, contrastingly	* Danny runs fast. Hanna, **on the other hand**, runs faster.	Contrast is achieved through using contrast words such as but etc. The construct consists of two facts that are compared and contrasted to each other.
13. Adverbial clause	* answered the wife **laughing.**	An independent clause that describes the modus in which the verb occurred: she answered while she was laughing.
14. Final clause	* They went to sleep late **for** they wanted to watch the match.	Usually are identifiable by words such as **for, aiming at, targeting.**

Tables of Graded Language Patterns

Linguistic constructs	Samples	Important notes
Phase B: 15. Direct speech, Indirect speech	* Mom told Tali, **"Picking mushrooms in the forest is forbidden."** * Mom told Tali **that** it is forbidden to pick mushrooms in the forest.	Direct speech construct is marked by the use of quotation marks and a comma that precedes it. Indirect construct is marked by the use of subordinating words such as **that, which, WH-words and more.**
16. Idioms	* Keep an eye on… Actions speak louder than words. * Leave you in the dust.	An idiom is a phrase or combination of words that their conclusive meaning is bigger than the separate meaning of each word on its own. There is an added value to the idiom. Usually the words are connected in a firm unchangeable way.
17. In order for + will (future)	* **In order** for you **to** achieve high grades in your exams, you must prepare for them.	In the construct "in order for" when it is used as a conditional phrase use auxiliary verbs like "must", "should" etc.
18. Conditional sentence	* If you had studied harder you would have succeeded.	**Would** in the protasis, the dependent clause that describes the condition; **will** in the apodosis, the independent. clausethat describes the consequences.
19. Comparatives–more, -er (nic**er**), less, as	* Ronny is smart**er than** I in math. * The new employee is **less** professional than the rest of us. * Daniel is **as** clever **as** his grandfather.	Comparatives usually set a comparison between two elements, usually by the use of *more, -er* (nicer) + **than**. In the construct *as… as* the idea of comparison is transferred without using than.

Tables of Graded Language Patterns

Linguistic constructs	Samples	Important notes
20. Superlative forms– Most + a superlative adjective Adjective + est Best, most	* The new movie is the **most successful** movie this summer. * It is the **funniest** movie I have ever seen.	Adjectives that are being used to convey an exaggeration.
21. Copulas	* Dogs are pets. * A tiger is a wild animal.	A copula links a subjective clause to the complement usually by using the verb *be* (is, are, was, were). The complement can be either a nominative, an adjectival or propositional clause.
22. Yes/no questions	* "Did you beat me?" yelled the hare to the tortoise.	A question whose answer can be either yes or no.
23. Either… or Neither… nor	* You can **either** run fast **or** try even harder but you're **neither** going to beat me **nor** are you going to win the victory cup.	**Either…or** is a pronoun and adverb signifying two possibilities. **Neither… nor** signifies the absence of both possibilities.

Table of Workbook 2 Texts and Skills

Skills \ Texts	The Maid	The Sparrow	The Three Counsels of the Rooster	Not to Shame	Small Fish, Big Fish	The Bundle of Sticks
Literal understanding						
Sequence	*	*	*		*	*
Locating details	*	*	*			*
Main idea	*	*		*	*	
Separating the wheat from the chaff	*	*	*		*	*
Mapping of concepts			*		*	
Raising and classifying questions	*				*	
Classifications (classification tables)	*		*			
Summarization			*			
Interpretive understanding						
Locating an implicit not-stated main idea		*	*	*		
Prediction of events	*	*	*			
Identifying the author's attitude	*					
Drawing conclusions and analyzing characters			*	*		
Implementation						
Distinguishing between opinions and facts	*					
Problem solving	*	*	*			
Language enrichment	*					
Alternative assessment						
Learning journal	*	*	*	*	*	*
Indicator	*	*	*	*	*	*